YOUR FIRST PET

TELLS HOW TO TAKE CARE OF:

636

- TWO GERBILS

- A GOLDEN HAMSTER

- TWO WHITE MICE

- A GUINEA PIG

- TWO GOLDFISH

- A SHELL PARAKEET

- A KITTEN

- A PUPPY

YOUR FIRST PET

AND HOW TO TAKE CARE OF IT

BY CARLA STEVENS
ILLUSTRATED AND BASED ON AN IDEA
BY LISL WEIL

READY-TO-READ
HANDBOOK

COLLIER BOOKS
Division of Macmillan Publishing Co., Inc.
New York
Collier Macmillan Publishers
London

Macmillan Publishing Co., Inc., 866 Third Ave., New York, N.Y. 10022
Collier Macmillan Canada, Ltd.
Your First Pet is published in a hardcover edition
by Macmillan Publishing Co., Inc.
Printed in the United States of America
First Collier Books edition 1978

10 9 8 7 6 5 4 3 2 1

LIBRARY OF CONGRESS CATALOGING IN PUBLICATION DATA

Stevens, Carla.
   Your first pet, and how to take care of it.
   (Ready-to-read handbook)
   Includes index.
   SUMMARY: Instructions for taking care of such household pets as gerbils, birds, mice, guinea pigs, hamsters, cats, dogs, and fish.
   1. Pets—Juvenile literature. [1. Pets]
I. Weil, Lisl. II. Title.
[SF416.2.S73 1978]   636.08'87   77-16585   ISBN 0-02-045240-3

CONTENTS

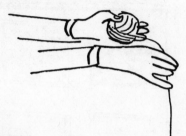

INTRODUCTION

You want a pet,
one that you can take care of yourself.
But what kind of pet?
Not a horse in the city, of course!
How about a gerbil
or a kitten or a guinea pig?
All the pets that this book tells about
can live comfortably indoors
if you take good care of them.
All except one. A dog.
Most dogs need freedom to run
and romp outdoors.

Still, you may want a small dog so much
that you will work very, very hard
to make a good life for him in the city.
The other pets in this book
are easier to take care of.
They are interesting and fun.
Read about them.
Go to a pet store and look at them.
Then before you make up your mind,
think about what it will mean to you
to own a living animal.

Remember that a pet cannot live
without you.
It cannot catch its own food to eat
or find its own water to drink.
It cannot clean its own cage or tank.
A pet is not a toy.
When you get tired of a toy,
you put it away and forget about it.
But you cannot ever forget your pet.
Your pet will need you, or someone like you,
to take care of it all of its life.

If you are sure that you can take
good care of an animal,
then it is time to choose your pet.

*   *   *

The four pets that you will read
about next are all small rodents.

Rodents have a special pair of
very sharp front teeth for gnawing.
These teeth are called incisors.
They will continue to grow
longer and longer
if the animal does not wear them down
by gnawing on seeds, nuts, wood,
and other hard objects.

Rodents can hear much better than people.
They can hear sounds so high
that humans cannot hear them.

They also have
a very good sense of smell.

Gerbils, hamsters, guinea pigs,
and mice live well indoors in cages.
They are good pets because they are
active and easy to take care of.

TWO GERBILS

A gerbil is a small, furry rodent.
He has a tuft of hair
at the tip of his long tail.
His natural home is in the deserts
of Asia, Africa, and eastern Europe.
Gerbils are gentle and easy to care for.
They are friendly and curious.
They will not bite unless you
frighten or hurt them.
Most rodents are nocturnal.
This means that they sleep
during the day and are awake at night.
Gerbils are not nocturnal.
They are active when you are.

Two gerbils will live
more happily together.
Buy two young gerbils
of the same sex from the same litter.
They probably will not fight.
If they do fight,
you will have to separate them.
You may even have to give one away.

A HOME FOR YOUR GERBILS

You will need:

> 10-gallon tank
> wire mesh lid
> food dish
> water bottle and holder
> 5-pound bag of wood shavings
> small juice can
>   with both ends removed

A large tank is a good home
for two gerbils.
The glass sides will protect them
from drafts.
Fill the tank with wood shavings
at least 4 inches deep.

In their natural home,
gerbils burrow underground.
In the home you make for them,
they will burrow in the shavings.
Gerbils are very good jumpers.
Always keep a book or something heavy
on each end of the wire mesh lid
to hold the lid down
so that the gerbils cannot escape.
Put a small juice can in the tank.
Your gerbils will play with the can
and sometimes sleep in it.

Fill the water bottle.
Turn it upside down and put it in the holder.
Hang the holder on the inside of the tank.

Your desk is a good place for the tank
because you can easily watch your gerbils.

The normal room temperature
of your house is good for the gerbils.
If it gets cool at night, they will
burrow in the shavings to keep warm.
Never, never put the tank
in direct sunlight.
The temperature might get so hot
inside the tank that it could kill them.

FEEDING YOUR GERBILS

boxed gerbil food   potato
sunflower seeds   carrot
apple   popcorn
celery

The gerbil food that comes in a box
from your pet store is a balanced diet
of seeds and grains.
A tablespoon of dry food each day
is enough for each gerbil.
Put the food in the food dish.

You will soon find out that your gerbils
always eat the sunflower seeds first.
But sunflower seeds contain a lot of fat.
Your gerbils might gain too much weight
if they eat nothing but sunflower seeds.
Use them as a treat.
Twice a week give your gerbils
a small piece of apple,
fresh celery, or carrot.
Your pets could get sick from
eating too many fresh greens.

CLEANING YOUR GERBILS' HOME

Gerbils have no odor. One reason is
that they drink very little water,
and so they excrete
only a few drops of urine a day.
If there are 4 or 5 inches of
wood shavings in the tank,
you will not have to clean
their home so often.
Once every three weeks is enough.
First find a good place to keep your
gerbils while you are cleaning the tank.
A tall cardboard box will do.
Put some seeds in the box
with your gerbils.
Then scoop
the wood shavings
out of the tank
and put them in
one or two large paper bags.
Put the bags in the garbage can.

Ask someone to help you carry the tank
into the bathroom. Put it in the tub.
Scrub the bottom of your tank
with soap and water.
Be sure to clean the corners.
They seem to get the dirtiest.

Then rinse the tank out with plain water.
Dry the tank thoroughly before
you carry it back to your room.
Put in clean bedding
and then your gerbils.
It is fun to watch them making
new tunnels. Finally, wash your hands!

PLAYING WITH YOUR GERBILS

Always close the door to your room
before you take your gerbils
out of the tank.
It won't be quite so hard
to find a lost gerbil in one room.
Be sure your gerbils are not sleeping
when you pick them up.
A sleeping gerbil
will become frightened if you wake him.
He might even try to bite you.
Put your hand underneath
the gerbil's body.
Wait a minute until your gerbil
gets used to your smell.
Then scoop him up gently.
Let him rest in the palm of your hand.
(His whiskers tickle!)

If he tries to scurry away, hold onto the
base of his tail with your other hand.
When he is quiet,
feed him a sunflower seed.
Then gently stroke him
behind the ears
or on his head.

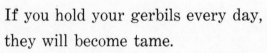

If you hold your gerbils every day,
they will become tame.
Put a few sunflower seeds in your pocket.
Let your gerbils know they are there.
If you do this every day for a few days,
your gerbils will begin to look for
their treats in your pocket!

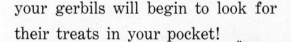

A GOLDEN HAMSTER

The golden hamster's natural home
is in the desert of Syria.
There he lives on insects, worms,
birds' eggs, seeds, and nuts.
A family of golden hamsters was
first captured more than 40 years ago
by a scientist who wanted to
use them in his laboratory.
Later, some people thought
they would make good pets.
Today there are more pet hamsters
than wild hamsters.
The golden hamster looks like
a tiny, furry teddy bear.
He has a very short tail.

A hamster is different from a gerbil
in several ways. He is nocturnal.
He has large cheek pouches
where he stores food or litter.
When they are filled, the pouches extend
all the way to the hamster's shoulders.

A hamster's front teeth are very sharp,
sharper than a gerbil's.

It is a good idea to buy only one young
hamster until you learn more about
the ways of these small animals.

A HOME FOR YOUR HAMSTER

You will need:

hamster cage at least 10 inches by 20 inches
exercise wheel
water bottle and holder
large juice can with one side removed
food dish
newspapers
bedding—wood shavings, hay,
   or hamster litter that comes in bags
wood to gnaw on
large piece of plastic or oil cloth

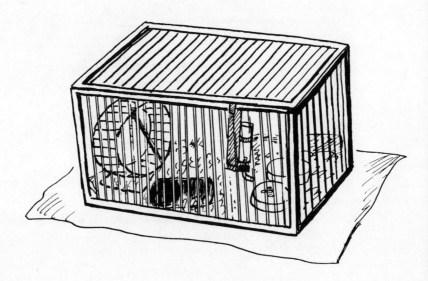

Your hamster cage has a pan
that can be removed for cleaning.
Put 3 or 4 layers of newspapers
on the bottom of the pan.
Let the newspapers extend up
around the sides.
Then fill the pan
with at least 2 inches of bedding.
The newspapers will help
to keep the bedding in the cage.

Some will still be tossed out
by your hamster.
A large piece of plastic or oil cloth
under the cage will protect
the table from the bedding.

Normal room temperature
is good for your hamster.
Don't leave the cage in direct sunlight.
Hamsters do not need a lot of sunshine.
Now you are ready to put your
hamster in the cage.
Don't try to pick him up
for a few days.
Let him get used
to his new home.

FEEDING YOUR HAMSTER

Your pet store sells dry hamster food
in 1-pound boxes.

Hamsters also like:

carrots	milk
lettuce	peanuts
celery	corn
potatoes	soybeans
apples	wheat germ oil
dry dog food	cod liver oil

Fill the water bottle and hang it
upside down on the inside of the cage.
Check each day to be sure that
there is water in the bottle.
Wash the inside of the
bottle once a week.

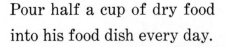

Pour half a cup of dry food
into his food dish every day.

Wash and dry the fruit and vegetables
to be sure that they are clean.
Don't give him too much.
Remember how small your hamster is.
Each day take out the fresh food that
your hamster did not eat the day before.
If you give your hamster more dry food
than he can eat at one time,
he will put it in his cheek pouches.
You will know when he is
hoarding his food.
His cheeks will be
very puffed out.
Try to watch when he
empties his pouches.
First he blows some food out of his mouth.
Then he presses forward against each side
of his neck with his front paws
until the rest of the food is forced out.
If he is hungry, he will eat
all the food he hoarded.

CLEANING THE HAMSTER CAGE

Clean your hamster's cage once a week.
First put your hamster in a safe place.
A large cardboard box will do.
Remove the bottom pan and dump
the soiled newspapers and shavings
into a large paper bag.
Put the paper bag into the garbage can.
Wash the pan with soap and water.
Scrub the corners with a brush.
Rinse the pan with plain water.
Dry it and slide it back into the cage.
Put clean newspapers on the bottom
and fresh shavings on the papers.
Wash and dry the juice can if you have one.
Finally, put back your hamster.

HANDLING YOUR HAMSTER

When your hamster is used to his
new home, you can begin to tame him.
It will take a lot of time.
You must pick him up every day.
If your hamster seems easily frightened,
it is a good idea to use gloves.
He might bite.
Put your hand slowly in the cage.
Let him sniff it.

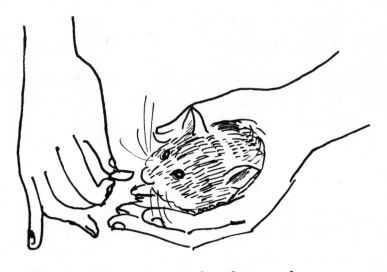

Then gently put your hand around
his back and under his body.
Lift him slowly and hold him firmly
so that he will not be afraid of falling.
Each time you pick him up,
give him something good to eat.
When you let your hamster out of his
cage, be sure that the door
to your room is closed.
If he escapes from your hand,
you might have a hard time catching him.

Hamsters like to crawl into dark places.
If you can't find your hamster, put his
cage on the floor where you last saw him.
Leave the door open and put food inside.
Then wait patiently until your hamster
is hungry enough to come for the food.
If he wasn't carrying a lot of food in
his cheek pouches, he will probably get
hungry by the time you are ready for bed.
When he enters his cage to eat, you will
have to be ready to close the door quickly.

TWO WHITE MICE

The mice in pet stores are almost tame.
They are easy to care for
and fun to watch.
They are very, very lively.
They are always climbing and exploring
or running in the exercise wheel.
The most common pet store mouse
is white.
But they come in other colors, too.
Mice that have different color patterns
are usually more expensive.
Buy two young mice of the same sex.

A HOME FOR YOUR MICE

You will need:

large mouse cage
(Be sure that it is at least 9 inches wide,
16 inches long, and 10 inches high.)
water bottle and holder
seed dispenser
exercise wheel
small juice can, or small box
with a hole for a door
cotton and string for a nest
wood to gnaw on (Remember that mice
are rodents and must wear down
their growing incisor teeth.)
newspapers
5-pound bag of wood shavings

Line the removable pan at the bottom of
the cage with 4 or 5 layers of newspapers.
Put in enough shavings
to cover the newspapers.
Hang the water bottle
on the inside of the cage.
Find a place away
from drafts for your cage.

A good place for it is on your desk.
If your room is cooler at night,
your little pets will curl up together
in their nest to keep warm.
If it gets very cool,
put a towel over the cage at night.

Be sure that it is an old towel, though.
Mice love to chew holes in cloth.
Change the toys in your cage
every once in a while.
Do you have a small truck
or some doll furniture?
Mice love to explore new toys.

FEEDING YOUR MICE

bird seed (It is good for your mice.)
bread crusts
dry dog food
lettuce
celery
carrots
sunflower seeds (Remember that they contain
too much fat to be given all the time.)

Throw away the hulls and fill the seed
dispenser with fresh seeds each day.
Check to see that the water bottle is filled.
Feed your mice a tiny, tiny piece of carrot
and a little piece of lettuce each day.

CLEANING THE MOUSE CAGE

Mouse droppings and urine have an
unpleasant odor.
That is why you must
change the newspapers in their cage
at least three times a week.
Once a week, wash the entire cage
with soap and water.
Before you begin to clean the cage,
put your mice in a safe place.
A large pail or box is a good place.

Scrub the removable tray
with soap and water.
Be sure to clean the corners.
Rinse the tray with water.
Dry it well before putting in
clean newspapers and shavings.
Put in clean cotton and string
so that your mice can build a new nest.
Always wash your hands after cleaning
your pets' cage.

HANDLING YOUR MICE

Your mice will become tame if you hold
them for a while every day.
Never pick up your mouse by her tail.
It hurts her.
Put your hand over her
and grasp her firmly
before you lift her.
Stroke her gently with your free hand.
Give her a sunflower seed as a treat.

A GUINEA PIG

A guinea pig is not a pig at all.
It is a rodent like the gerbil,
the hamster, and the mouse.
Perhaps he got the "pig" part
of his name because his funny whistle
is like the squeal of a pig.
The guinea pig is not as active
as a hamster or a gerbil.
But he is very friendly and gentle.

Before you buy a guinea pig,
look at the different kinds
in the pet store.
The Peruvian has long hair.
If you buy a Peruvian guinea pig,
you will have to brush his coat
every day to keep it clean.
The Abyssinian
also has long hair,
but the coat is formed
into many rosettes.
It must be brushed daily, too.
The short-haired kind is called English.
English guinea pigs
are easiest to keep clean.
If you want to have your guinea pig
for a long time, buy a young one.

A HOME FOR YOUR GUINEA PIG

Your guinea pig does not need a large
cage, because he is not very active.
A cage 2 feet long and 1 foot wide
is large enough for him.
It does not have to have high sides.
Guinea pigs cannot jump.
The bottom of the cage should have
a pan that you can take out and clean.
And your guinea pig needs
a little house to sleep in.
It does not have to have a floor.
Three sides and a top are enough.

Your guinea pig also needs
a water bottle and holder
and a dispenser for his dry food.

Shavings
or kitty litter
or hay
are good for his bedding.
Don't be surprised
if he eats some of the hay!
Always put 4 to 6 layers of
newspapers on the bottom of the pan
before you put in the bedding.
Two inches of bedding is enough.
It is very important that you find
a good place for the cage.
It must not get much cooler
than 70 degrees.
And it should not be drafty.
Guinea pigs catch colds more easily
in rooms that are not warm enough.
If your room gets cool at night,
cover the cage with a blanket.
Be sure that your pet's nest box
has bedding in it to keep him warm.

Never put the cage in direct sunlight
without putting a sheet or a towel over it
so that there will be shade for your pet.
Your guinea pig cannot stand
too much heat.

FOOD FOR YOUR GUINEA PIG

You will soon find out that
your guinea pig loves to eat!
Every time you pass by the cage,
he will squeal at you.
He wants you
to give him a treat.

Here is a list of the foods
that are good for him
and that he likes to eat:

guinea pig pellets
(They contain grains and minerals
and vitamins that he needs.)
fresh, leafy greens—
lettuce, carrot tops, spinach,
clover, dandelion leaves
carrots, celery, apples, tomatoes

Keep a supply of pellets in the dispenser.
Your guinea pig will nibble at them often.
Change his water each day.
Feed him greens and fruit once a day.
Be sure that the greens are clean and dry.
Take out all fruits or vegetables that
get dirty or wet on the bottom of the cage.
They can make your guinea pig sick.

CLEANING THE CAGE

Your guinea pig will make a mess!
Change the newspapers and litter
three times a week.
Be sure you wash the pan with
soap and water once a week.
Scrub the corners well.
Dry the pan before putting in
clean newspapers and litter.

PLAYING WITH YOUR GUINEA PIG

Play with your pet every day.
He will become very tame.
Scratch him under his chin
and on his head.

He will learn to like being petted.
When you pick up your guinea pig,
be very careful that you don't drop him.
Always use two hands to hold him.
You can see how short his legs are
and how fat and round his body is.
If he fell even a very short distance,
he would hurt himself.

Sit on the floor when you play with him.
Then there is no chance that he can fall.
A guinea pig is good company!

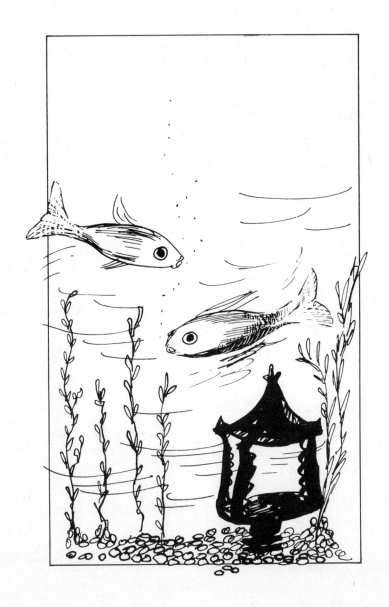

TWO GOLDFISH

You cannot hold and pet goldfish, but you
will enjoy watching these graceful fish swim.
There are many kinds of goldfish.
You can pay 50 cents for the common
variety or over 100 dollars for a rare kind.
Some kinds of goldfish have long,
flowing tails. Some are black.
Others have large, bulgy eyes.
If you have never taken care of fish before,
buy two common goldfish or two comets.
The comet looks like the common goldfish
except that it has a longer tail fin.
Both the common goldfish
and the comet are very hardy.
Their fins are not as delicate
as other long-finned goldfish.

A HOME FOR YOUR GOLDFISH

The best home for two goldfish
is a 10-gallon fish tank.
Your goldfish need more space
than other aquarium fish.
Like animals, all fish must breathe
oxygen in order to live.
The oxygen they breathe
is dissolved in water.
Some of the oxygen in the water
comes from the air.
If your tank has
a large surface exposed to air,
more oxygen reaches the water.

A goldfish bowl is not a good home
for goldfish. The neck of the bowl
is too small. Very little of the
water surface is exposed to the air.

When you buy your tank, also buy:
  tank lid
  feeding ring
  dip tube
  siphon
  two 2-gallon pails
  three 5-pound bags of gravel
  six water plants (Ask for sagittaria.
    Goldfish will not nibble them
    as readily as other plants.)
  goldfish food (Buy several different kinds:
    dried, frozen, and the pastes.)

Before you fill your tank with water,
you should rinse the inside, even if
it is new. A good place to rinse out
your tank is in the bathtub.
Your tank is heavy, so ask someone
to help you to move it.
Be sure you both lift it
by grasping the bottom corners.
Clean it with a brush or a cloth.
Then dry it.
Next, rinse the gravel, a bag at a time.
Put the gravel in a pot under a
running faucet. Stir the gravel in the
bottom of the pot with your fingers.
When the water is clear,
you know the gravel is clean.

Now think carefully where you want
to put your tank. You cannot move it
easily after it is filled with water.
The best place for your goldfish
is on a table near a window.
Goldfish need good light
but not too much sunlight.
Too much sun can also cause
tiny plants called algae
to grow in the tank.
They turn the water green.
If the water in the tank turns green,
the tank is getting too much sunlight.
Cover the sunny side and top of the tank
with large sheets of cardboard.
In a few days, the algae will disappear.

When your tank is in a good place,
pour all the gravel into it.
Move the gravel so that there is
more along the back of the tank.
Now the time has come
to fill your tank with water.
Use one of your pails to carry the water.
Put a cup on the gravel in the tank.
If you pour the water slowly
into the cup first, the gravel will
not be disturbed by flowing water.
When your tank is half full,
you are ready to plant.
Make holes in the deeper gravel
with your finger. Put a plant in each hole.
Then cover the roots with gravel.

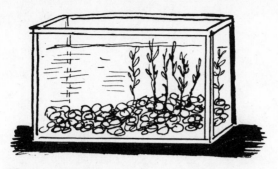

Be sure to cover only the roots of
your plants. If you cover the leaves too,
they will turn brown and die.
When your tank is filled with water,
it is almost ready for your goldfish.
Almost, but not quite.
In the city, water from your faucet
contains chemicals that keep it pure
for you to drink.
One chemical is a gas called chlorine.
Chlorine is not good for fish.
If you leave water standing
in the tank for several days,
the chlorine will evaporate
into the air.
The water will also be
the same temperature as your room.

Although goldfish can live in very cold water,
they prefer water between 60 and 80 degrees.
Always keep a pail of water near the tank.
The water will be just right
for the tank when you need it.
Now it is time to buy your goldfish.
You will probably bring them home
in a plastic bag
filled with water.

Float the bag in the tank for an hour
so that the temperature in the bag
and the tank will be the same.
Open the bag and let the fish swim out.
At first they will be frightened.
It takes time for them
to get used to their new home.

FEEDING YOUR GOLDFISH

There are many different foods
that you can buy for your goldfish.
There are dried and frozen foods,
pellets, pastes, and live foods.
Try them all.
That is the best way to find out
which foods your goldfish prefer.
If your goldfish lived wild in a pond,
they would catch and eat insects,
worms, and other small water animals.
Your goldfish will be much more active
if they can catch and eat live food
in their tank home.
Buy live foods such as
brine shrimp and
fruit flies in your pet store
and feed them to your fish
at least once a week.

Feed your goldfish once a day.
Put the food inside the feeding ring.
They will come to the ring to be fed.
It also keeps the food in one place.
Give them a tiny, tiny bit of food.

When they have eaten it, give them
a little more, and then a little more
for about five minutes.
Do not give your fish too much food.
Overfeeding can kill them.
Take out all uneaten food
with your dip tube.

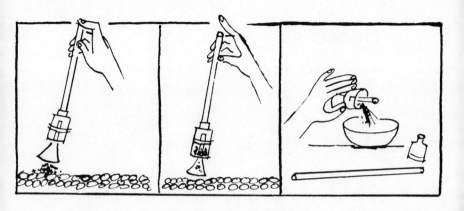

A dip tube is a long glass tube
with a bulge in the glass at one end.
Put your finger over
the narrow end of the tube.
Then put the tube into the tank.
Place it over the food.
Take your finger off the end.
The food will be sucked up into
the bulge of the glass tube.
Put your finger over the narrow end
of the tube again
and lift it out of the tank.
Empty the food into a bowl or glass.
Pour the contents into the toilet.

CLEANING THE TANK

Vacuum clean the bottom of your tank
with a siphon once a week.
A piece of rubber or plastic tubing
about 4 or 5 feet long
and ¼ or ⅜ inches in diameter
will make a good siphon.
Fill the tubing with water.
Close each end with a finger.

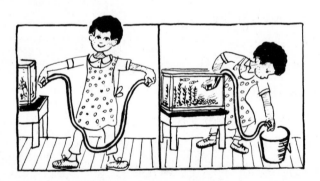

Put one end of the tubing in the tank.
Put the other end in a
large empty pail on the floor.
Take your fingers off both ends
of the tubing at the same time.

The water will begin to flow
through the tubing out of the tank
into the pail.
Be careful not to touch your fish
with the tubing.
Try not to suck up any gravel either.
When the bottom is clean,
pull the tubing out of the tank.
Pour the water in the pail into the sink.
You must replace the water that
you removed from the tank.
Use the water that has been
standing in your other pail.
Pour it very slowly against the glass
wall so that the rest of the tank water
is not disturbed.

Then fill your pail so that you will have
conditioned water when you
clean your tank again.
After you have had your goldfish
for a while, you might want to add
more fish to your tank.
If you add more fish, you must be sure
that there is enough oxygen in the water
for them to survive.
One way to be sure is to force air
into the tank water by means of a pump.
The air bubbles that rise to the surface
also help to increase the amount of
water that is exposed to the air.
This is called aerating the tank.

More fish will also add more wastes.
A mechanical filter will help
to keep the water clear.
There are several kinds.
The filter that hangs on the outside
of the tank is easiest to clean.
Water is pumped through a tube
into a box containing glass wool and
charcoal and then back into the tank.
When the glass wool becomes dirty,
replace it with clean wool.
Your pet shop dealer will suggest
a good air pump and filter.
You will probably
need help to set
them up so that
they work properly.

A SHELL PARAKEET

If you like birds,
you will enjoy having a parakeet.
You can tame a young parakeet easily.
He will learn to sit on your finger.
If you are patient,
you can teach him to talk.
When you go to buy a parakeet, plan
to spend some time at the pet store.
Look for a young parakeet.
He should be from 6 to 12 weeks old.
A young bird will have shell-like
markings on its forehead above the cere.
The cere is the swelling at the base of
the upper bill around the nostril holes.

A male's cere is blue.

A female's cere is tan or brownish.

The markings on the forehead
will disappear when your parakeet
grows older.

Decide on the parakeet you like best.

But be sure that his feathers are bright
and that he moves around actively.

Some people think male birds are easier
to train to talk.

A HOME FOR YOUR PARAKEET

There are all kinds of cages
for parakeets.

Buy the largest cage you can afford.

It should be at least 9 inches wide,
18 inches long, and 13 inches high.

You will also need:

> feeding cup and water cup
> two or three perches that are
>   different shapes if possible
>   (The different shapes will keep
>   your bird's feet from remaining
>   too long in one position.)
> swinging perch
> plastic or glass guards for the sides
>   (to keep seed and gravel from
>   being scattered out of the cage)
> bell
> bird bath
> paper to fit the sliding tray
>   at the bottom of the cage
> cover for your cage

Put your bird where he will get used
to having people around him.
The cage should be placed in a part of
your room where there are no drafts
or sudden changes in temperature.
Do not put him in the kitchen, though.
Birds are very sensitive to smells.
Even the faintest odor from a gas stove
might make him sick.
Also, a hot stove can be dangerous
if your parakeet escapes from his cage.
Cover his cage at night.

If your parakeet lived out-of-doors,
he would go to sleep when the sun goes
down and awaken when the sun comes up.
A cover that darkens his cage will help
your pet to get the rest he needs.
When the room is cooler at night,
it will also keep the cage warm.

FEEDING YOUR PARAKEET

parakeet seed

It is important to have fresh seed,
so do not buy too much at any one time.

a cuttlebone

This is the dried shell of a cuttle fish.
It is almost pure lime.
Lime is a form of calcium.
Calcium helps to build a strong beak
and good bones.

A parakeet's beak continues to grow
just like your fingernails.
Your parakeet will wear down
and at the same time
sharpen his beak
against the cuttlebone.
He also flakes off tiny bits
of the bone and eats them.

greens—lettuce, carrot tops,
spinach, dandelions

The greens should be fed 3 times a week.
Be sure they are fresh.
Wash them to remove any dirt or insect
spray that might be on them.
Do not put the greens on the cage floor.
They will get dirty from your bird's droppings.
Tie the greens to the inside
of the cage with a piece of string.

gravel

A parakeet has no teeth.
He must have gravel
to help him digest his food.
Put some gravel on the cage floor.

Polyvisol, a vitamin in liquid form

Add 1 drop to the drinking water
once a week.

CLEANING THE CAGE

Change the paper on the bottom
of the pan three times a week.

Don't forget to put clean gravel
on the paper.

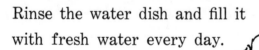

Rinse the water dish and fill it
with fresh water every day.

Clean out the seed dish every day
even if it looks full.
You will be surprised to find that
there are many hulls in the dish.
Wash and dry it
before adding more seeds.

Once a month, the cage should get
a thorough cleaning.
Wait until your pet is tame enough
to fly around your room.
Then you can let him out
while you are scrubbing the cage.
Be sure that you have closed
all the doors and windows, though!
A good place to wash the cage
is in the bathtub.

Closed

Scrub the cage all over with soap
and water. Wash the toys and scrub
the perches, too. Rinse everything.
(You can use the shower!)
Finally, dry the cage well.
A damp cage could make your bird sick.
By this time, your pet will be
hungry enough to fly back to his cage.
If he has left droppings
around the room, wait until they dry.
Then sweep them up
with dustpan and brush.
There is usually no stain left.

FINGER-TRAINING YOUR PARAKEET

The best time of day to train
your pet is at night.
If he gets frightened and flies
out of your hand before he is tame,
it will be easier to catch him.
Watch where he lands, then turn out
the light. Birds do not fly in the dark.
Hold your parakeet gently but firmly
with both hands. Do not squeeze him.
Stroke his head with one of your fingers
and talk to him.

When he stops struggling,
put him back in his cage.
For the first week, put your hand slowly
in the bird's cage and gently
stroke his chest with your finger.

When he gets used to your hand,
push your finger up against his chest.
He will have to climb onto your finger
or fall off his perch.
Lift him slowly out of his cage.
Walk around the room
talking softly to him.

Think of a word like "up" or "come"
to use each time
you push against his chest.
Eventually, whenever you say,
"Up, Pete," or "Come, Harry,"
he will step onto your finger.

TEACHING YOUR PET TO TALK

Remember that parakeets
don't really understand
what they are saying
when they talk.
They are only repeating sounds
they have heard over and over.

That's why it takes a lot of time
to teach your pet to talk.
You may have to work with him
every day for three months before
he will repeat what you say.
The important thing is not to give up.
He will learn best if only you teach him.
At first, work with him
in the early evening
when he is quiet and ready for rest.
Leave him in his cage.
Stand at one side and very slowly
and clearly repeat his name
for about five minutes.

Do this day after day.
Then one day you may be rewarded!

After your parakeet has learned
his name, you can begin to teach him
a phrase such as "Hello, Dolly,"
or "Come here, Tony."
The more he learns, the easier it is
for him to imitate your voice.
He might even learn up to 20
or 30 single words and phrases.

A BATH

A parakeet keeps himself clean by
preening his feathers with his bill.
Usually, he is not too fond of taking baths.
You can find out whether your parakeet
likes baths by putting the bird bath filled
with water in the bottom of the cage.
Put some gravel in the bottom
of the bird bath, so that he won't slip.

MITES

If your pet scratches a lot,
he may have mites.
Mites are tiny, bloodsucking insects
that are found on many birds.
A good way to check for mites
is to cover the cage at night.
A white flannel cloth is best.
If you see tiny red moving spots
on the cloth in the morning,
your bird has mites.
Take your bird to a veterinarian.
He will examine your pet and
if necessary give you medicine for him.

A KITTEN

A kitten is a good pet for the city.
He will not be unhappy
in an apartment.
He will get enough exercise climbing
onto high shelves, exploring all the
dark closets, and playing with you!
It is a big responsibility for you
to raise a kitten.
Because he is not kept in a cage,
it is up to you to keep him safe.
If you live on a high floor,
an open window can be dangerous
for your kitten.
Make sure there are screens
to protect him from falling out.

When your kitten comes to live
with you, he should not be less
than 8 weeks old.
If he can be left with his mother
until he is 8 weeks old,
or even older, he will get used
to his new home more easily.

There are two things you must have
for your kitten when he arrives:
a place to sleep and a litter pan.
The place to sleep can be a basket
with a soft piece of blanket or wool or
a cardboard box with one side removed
so that he can get in easily.

Help him to know that
this is his special place.
Put him in it when he is sleepy
and stroke him gently until he purrs.
You can buy litter and a litter pan
from your pet store.
Litter absorbs wetness and odors.
It is sold in 10- and 25-pound bags.
Fill the pan with at least 4 inches
of litter. Put the pan inside a large
cardboard box. Leave the top of the box
and one side open.
When cats dig their holes and bury their
droppings, sometimes they spread
the litter all over.
The sides of the box will keep the litter
from spilling out of the pan
onto the floor.

A good place for the litter pan
is in the corner of your bathroom
or kitchen. Put your kitten
in the pan after he eats.
It takes only a day or two for him
to learn to use the pan whenever
he has to go to the bathroom.

A kitten feels soft and furry.
You will be tempted to carry him around
in your arms all day.
Love him and keep him company.
But try not to hold him too much.
Kittens can become very nervous
and are easily frightened
if they are handled too much.

When you do pick up your kitten,
put one hand under his chest.
Put your other hand under his rear
and lift him gently.
Support his whole body when you
hold him. You can hurt a kitten
if you do not pick him up properly.

As soon as you can, take him to
your veterinarian for a checkup.
Your vet will look him over carefully
to be sure that he is healthy.
He will give him shots
to protect him from cat diseases.

FEEDING YOUR KITTEN

Your kitten should be fed
three times a day, from 8 weeks on.
From 6 months on, two meals
a day are enough for your cat.
Dry cat food in bags that you can buy
from your grocery store
contains the proper balance of protein,
vitamins, and minerals for cats.
It also costs less than canned cat food
and it is easy to keep in your kitchen.
Cats do not overeat.
When your kitten is full,
he will stop eating.
How much should you feed
your kitten at one meal?
You will have to experiment.

Try giving him ½ cup of dry food.
Moisten it with ¼ cup of warm milk.
If he eats every bit and looks for more,
increase the amount you give him
next time. If he doesn't finish,
cover his dish.
Put it in the refrigerator
until his next meal.
If you leave it on the floor,
the milk may turn sour.
You would not like to have exactly
the same meal three times a day,
day after day after day.
Cats are the same way.
Vary his meals by giving him cooked
mackerel, or chicken or liver, kidneys
or heart at one meal every few days.
Also, cooked vegetables mixed in with
the meat are good for your kitten.
No bones, please!

Be sure that you cut the food into tiny
pieces. His baby teeth are sharp
but very, very small. Don't forget to give
your kitten warm milk three times a day.
And you should always have a dish of
fresh water on the floor for your kitten
to drink when he is thirsty.

SCRATCHING

A cat must have something to scratch.
If he does not scratch, his claws will
grow so long that he will have trouble
walking. If your kitten lived outdoors,
he would claw the trunks of trees.
Indoors, he claws rugs
and furniture.
And no matter how
often you scold him,
you won't stop him.

The best you can do is to give him
something of his own to scratch.
Pet stores sell scratching posts.
If your pet still scratches furniture,
rub some catnip on the scratching post.
Cats love catnip!

CLEANING THE LITTER PAN

Buy a large long-handled kitchen spoon
with holes. Use it to remove the droppings
from the litter pan every day.
Flush the droppings down the toilet.
If you remove them, you won't
have to change the litter so often.
Once a week is probably often enough.

When the litter begins to smell of urine,
empty it into a paper bag.
Put the paper bag in the garbage can.
Wash the pan with soap and water.
Rinse and dry the pan well
before putting in fresh litter.

PLAYING WITH YOUR KITTEN

Kittens love to play.
Playing is good exercise for your kitten.
Ask your mother for a piece of yarn
or string. Crumple up a sheet of paper.
Tie the yarn to one end. Then pull
the paper slowly across the floor.
Watch your kitten pounce!

Put a paper bag on the floor.
When your kitten explores inside,
tap the outside of the bag
with a pencil (not too hard!).
It looks funny to see a paper bag
jumping around on the floor.
You will think of many other games
to play with your kitten.
Remember though, he is only a baby.
Don't tire him by playing
with him too much.
Don't give him sharp toys
that could hurt him.

A PUPPY

A city apartment is not
a proper home for most dogs.
Still, if you want a dog very much
and your parents will let you have one,
choose a puppy that will grow up
to be a small dog.
A small dog can get enough exercise
running and playing in your apartment.
Choose a puppy that has short hair.
It will not shed as much as a long-haired dog.
Buy a puppy that is about 7 weeks old.
Or you can get one free
from an animal shelter.

When you are at school,
someone will have to feed her lunch
and change her newspapers
when she goes to the bathroom.
Have your puppy checked over
by a veterinarian as soon as possible.
He will give your puppy shots to
protect her from certain dog diseases.
He will give you good advice
about what to feed her and how much.

A NAME FOR YOUR PUPPY

It won't take you long to think of
a good name for your puppy.
Pick a short name, one that will not
get mixed up with important words

you will use to train her—for example,
words like "no" or "heel" or "sit"
or "come." Use her name every time
you talk to your puppy. Remember that
a word is only a sound to a dog.
She will learn to come to the sound
of the word you use for her name.

HOLDING YOUR PUPPY

Puppies don't like to be
carried around.

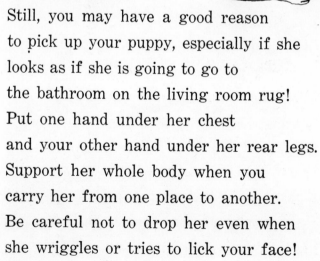

Still, you may have a good reason
to pick up your puppy, especially if she
looks as if she is going to go to
the bathroom on the living room rug!
Put one hand under her chest
and your other hand under her rear legs.
Support her whole body when you
carry her from one place to another.
Be careful not to drop her even when
she wriggles or tries to lick your face!

A BED FOR YOUR PUPPY

Your puppy should have her own bed.
It can be a cardboard box with
the top and one side removed.
Or you can buy a dog bed in a pet store.
Put something soft on the bottom,
like an old blanket or pillow. Put the
bed in a place that is not drafty. If she
sleeps in your bedroom, you should put
newspapers on the floor beside her bed.
She may have to go to the bathroom.
If she sleeps in a room by herself, she
may bark or howl because she is lonely.
Try putting a ticking clock near her bed
and a hot water bottle under her blanket.

FEEDING YOUR PUPPY

Dry dog food is cheaper than
canned food. It is just as nutritious.
You can save money if you buy
a 25-pound bag instead of a 5-pound bag.
On the outside of the bag there are
directions for feeding a dog
according to its weight.
Learn how much to feed your puppy.
Dogs can get sick from eating too much.
You can find out how much your puppy
weighs if you have a bathroom scale.
If your puppy won't sit still on the scale,
hold her in your arms
and weigh yourself and
your puppy together.
Then let her go and
weigh just yourself.
Subtract your weight
from what you both weigh.
The difference is her weight.

Puppies need to eat often.
From the time she is weaned from
her mother until she is 3 months old,
your puppy should have three meals a day.
When she is 6 months old,
two meals are enough.
After she is a year old,
one large meal a day is enough for her.
Moisten the dry food with milk.
Your vet might suggest adding
fresh meat to the dry food.
He might also want your puppy
to take vitamins.
Remember to keep fresh water in a bowl
so that she can drink when she is thirsty.
Always wash her bowl with soap and water
and then rinse it before putting food in it.

Don't leave leftover food in the dish.
Throw it away.
Next time give her less food.
Do not give her candy or other sweets.
Do not give her any water or food
after she has had her evening meal.
Then she probably won't have to go
to the bathroom
during the night.

HOUSEBREAKING YOUR PUPPY

A puppy has to go to the bathroom
very often. She usually has to go
after she drinks, after each of her
three meals, and sometimes even more often.
It is hard to take her outdoors
whenever she has to go.

That is why it is a good idea to have
a special place for her to go indoors.
A good place is in a corner of your
bathroom or in the hall.
Buy a large cookie tray. Put about
6 layers of newspapers on the tray.
Put your puppy on the papers
after every meal and whenever
she looks as if she has to go.
(You can tell, when she begins to sniff
around in circles or whine.)
When the newspapers become soiled,
roll them up and put them
in the garbage can.
Put clean papers on the tray.

At first, your puppy will make mistakes.
If you see her making a mistake,
say "No, no!" and carry her quickly
over to her tray.
If you don't see her, don't scold her
because it is too late.
She won't understand
what you are scolding her for.
If your puppy goes to the bathroom
on the floor or on the rug,
clean it as soon as possible.

Wash the spot with soap and water.
Rinse it with water.
Then wipe it with two tablespoons
of vinegar in a cup of water.
It will help to get rid of the smell.

A city sidewalk is not a good place for your dog to go to the bathroom. When you see a sign saying "Curb your dog," that means you must lead her to the street alongside the sidewalk.

TOYS FOR YOUR PUPPY

Your puppy needs to chew on things
in order to develop strong teeth.
But not your shoes or socks
or the legs of chairs and tables.
A large round beef bone is good to chew.
So is an old leather shoe.
Other chewing toys that you can buy
are made of hard rubber or dried leather.

TEACHING YOUR PUPPY TO OBEY YOU

When your puppy gets used to her new
home, you can begin to teach her to obey.
It is useful to have your puppy
learn to obey the words
"come," "sit," "heel," and "lie down."
Teach only one command at a time.
The first command you should
teach your puppy to obey is "come."
Give her a series of short lessons,
each about five minutes long.
Put your puppy on one side of your room.
Walk quickly to the other side.
Then call her.
Say "come" clearly several times.

At first, she will not understand.
She might look at you in a puzzled way.
If she starts sniffing around, sit her
down and quickly move away from her.
Repeat the word "come" with her name.
Eventually, she will come to you.
When she does, it is very important
that you pet her and praise her.
Then walk away from her again quickly.
Turn and say "come."
Repeat the word until she does come.
Praise her again. That ends the lesson.
But you may have to give this lesson
over and over for a few weeks
before she will understand
what you expect of her.

Never scold her or punish her
if she doesn't learn quickly.
Remember that she is only a baby.

LEARNING TO BEHAVE

Some puppies have to learn not to bark
too much, not to jump up on people,
not to beg for food, not to whine
and howl when left alone.
That is why the word "no" is an important
word sound for your puppy to learn.
It means that she is to stop doing
whatever she is doing.

The tone of your voice should help
to make her understand
that you really mean what you say.
If scolding her does not stop her, then
you might have to fold a newspaper
and slap her once or twice on her rump.
The slapping noise will frighten her.

Never, never hit your puppy with
your hand or with a stick.
Never hit your puppy on the head.
Don't punish her too often.
Too much scolding
will confuse and frighten her.
She will forget all the things she learned.

PLAYING WITH YOUR PUPPY

There are three important reasons
why you should play with your puppy.
One is to give her exercise.
If she doesn't get enough exercise,
your puppy will grow fat and lazy.
A fat dog is not a healthy dog.
The second reason to play with your
puppy is that it is a lot of fun.
The third reason is that it is a good
way to let her know that you love her.
The more you love her
and are kind to her
and pay attention to her,
the more she will love you back.

MORE ABOUT YOUR PETS AND THEIR NEEDS

KEEPING YOUR PET'S CAGE CLEAN

Remember that your pet lives
all of his life in a small space.
He cannot move to a new home
when his cage becomes damp and dirty.
If you follow the directions in this book
for keeping your pet's cage clean,
he will not want to move.
Once a month, it is a good idea to clean
the cage with a liquid disinfectant.
(Once every other month for your gerbils.)
A disinfectant will kill any germs
that soap and water has not killed.

111

Sometimes liquid disinfectants are
so strong that they can burn your skin.
That is why it is important
to ask an older person to help you
when it is time to use one.
Pour a tablespoon of disinfectant
into a quart of water.
After you scrub the cage,
rinse it well with plain water.
Then dry it and put in clean bedding.

SOME ADVICE ABOUT WATER BOTTLES

You can have trouble
with your water bottle.
Sometimes a water bottle will leak if the
rubber stopper is not on tight or if
the angle of the tube is not quite right.

Check to be sure that water is not
slowly dripping out of the bottle.
Sometimes water does not come out of
a full bottle even when it is upside down.
Do not fill your water bottle
all the way to the top.
If you do not leave some space for air,
the water may not run down the tube.
Turn the bottle upside down and shake
it before you put it in the holder.

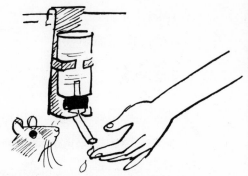

Check each day
to be sure that
the water can run
down the tube.
Tap the end of the tube several times
with your fingertip.
Is there water on your finger? If so,
then the bottle is working properly.

BITING

Almost all animals bite
when they are frightened.
It is their way of protecting themselves.
All the pets in this book can bite.
Even goldfish can bite.
Not you, of course, but one another.
When you pick up a small animal,
never grab it.
Scoop it slowly and gently
into the palm of your hand.
Imagine how you would feel
if a giant picked you up suddenly!
Never pick up a sleeping animal.
He is sure to be frightened
by being awakened too quickly.

If your pet bites you accidentally
and you bleed a little,
tell a grownup right away.
Wash the bite with soap and water.
Let someone put an antiseptic on it.
The person who helps you
may also want to call a doctor
to find out if there is anything else
to be done to prevent an infection.
After you have cared for your bite,
try to think why your pet bit you.
Did you frighten him
by picking him up too suddenly?
Does he have a sore that
hurts when you touch him?
Were you teasing him?
Or playing too rough?

Try to imagine what your pet was feeling. Remember that he doesn't *want* to bite you. He is defending himself against being hurt. Or, if he is very small, he is afraid of being caught and eaten.

WHEN YOUR PET GETS SICK

Animals get sick just as people do, sometimes for no apparent reason. You can tell when your pet is sick. He will look and behave differently. You will know something is wrong if he has runny eyes, sniffles, or diarrhea, or lies quietly refusing to eat or drink.

If you or your parents have not had
a lot of experience caring for animals,
it is a good idea to take your sick pet
to the veterinarian to be checked.
When you are sick, wash your hands
before you handle
your pet's food and water.
Do not pick up your pet
or play with him
until you are well again.

RAISING FAMILIES OF PETS

After you have had your pet for a while,
you might want to buy a mate for it.
A male and a female will usually have
a family within a short time.
But before you decide to breed your pet,
think about what it will mean to have
more animals in your home,
even for a little while.
If your pet is a rodent, the cage
must be large enough to hold a family.

Are you sure that you can find a home
for the babies when they are old enough
to leave their mother?
Do you have friends who want them?
Will your pet store take them?
Baby animals are very interesting.
They grow rapidly.
If you watch them every day,
you can almost see them growing.
There are books that tell how to breed
and raise all the animals in this book.

HOW LONG WILL YOUR PET LIVE?

The average life of each of the animals described in this book is:

cat	15 years
dog	12 years
gerbil	4 years
goldfish	10 years
guinea pig	4–5 years
hamster	2 years
parakeet	10 years
white mice	2 years

You can see that none of the pets
will live as long as you.
If your pet mouse dies
at the end of two years,
you shouldn't feel too sad.
She probably has died of old age.
It is always hard to lose a pet
you have grown to love.
But if you had fun taking care of
and playing with your pet,
the best thing to do is to get another.

INDEX